Start Reading
AND WRITING

D0418305

Stroke
the Cat

For Daniel, Natalie and Charlotte

First published in the UK in 2004 by
QED Publishing
A Quarto Group Company
226 City Road
London, EC1V 2TT

www.qed-publishing.co.uk

A Catalogue record for this book is available from the British Library.

ISBN 1 84538 325 7

Written by Wes Magee
Designed by Alix Wood
Editor Hannah Ray
Illustrated by Pauline Siewert

Series Consultant Anne Faundez
Creative Director Louise Morley
Editorial Manager Jean Coppendale

Printed and bound in China

Stroke the Cat

A collection of poems by Wes Magee

QED Publishing

Stroke the Cat

Stroke the cat,
stroke the cat
and lift it from the floor.

Stroke the cat,
stroke the cat
and shake hands with its paw.

Stroke the cat,
stroke the cat
and scratch its head once more.

Stroke the cat,
stroke the cat
– then **shoo** it through the door!

In My Garden

There's a cat in my garden
with a wasp on her toes.
    Shake it off,
     shake it off.
Look,
     there
        it
         goes!

Wazzzzzzzzzzzzzzzzzzzzzz

There's a dog in my garden
with a bee on his nose.
    Shake it off,
     shake it off.
Look,
     there
        it
         goes!

Buzzzzzzzzzzzzzzzzzzzzzz

Playtime

Children creeping,
children peeping,
children leaping, leaping, leaping.

Children teasing,
children wheezing,
children sneezing, sneezing, sneezing.

Children calling,
children falling,
children bawling, bawling, bawling.

Children hopping,
Children flopping.

There goes the bell!

Children,
    children,
        children
            stopping.

Climb the Mountain

Climb the mountain high,
touch the clouds and see the sky.
Feel the wind against you blow,
see the fields far far below.

← (Start here)

Animal Chat

Dogs growl,
Wolves howl.
  Cows moo,
  Doves coo.
Lions roar,
Crows caw.
  Horses neigh,
  Donkeys bray.
Monkeys shriek,
Mice squeak.
  Parrots squawk
  ... and I talk.

9

My Dog's First Poem
(To be read in a dog's voice)

My barking drives them
    up the wall.
I chew the carpet
    in the hall.
I love to chase
    a bouncing ... **banana**?

Everywhere I leave
    long hairs.
I fight the cushions
    on the chairs.
Just watch me race
    right up the ... **shower**?

Once I chewed
    a stick of chalk.
I get bored when
    the family talk.
Then someone takes me
    for a ... **wheelbarrow**?

My Teachers

My teacher's name
  is Mrs Large.
She's helped
  by Mrs Small.

Miss Thin comes in
  and she pins up
our paintings
  on the wall.

Big Mr Bigg's
  the music man,
and he takes us
  in the Hall.

There are
  so **many** teachers,
and I really like
  them all.

Yellow Boots

We're wearing yellow boots
    and the rain has stopped a-thumping.
We're wearing yellow boots
    and now we're puddle jumping!

We're wearing yellow boots
    and the rain has stopped a-lashing.
We're wearing yellow boots
    and now we're puddle splashing!

Dressing Up

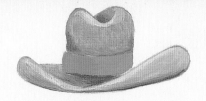

Ben can be a Pirate,
and Faye can be a Clown.
Hal can be a Postman
walking round the town.

Meena can be a Princess,
and Mitch can be a Knight.
Fran can be a Monster
and give us all a **fright**!

Ahmed can be a Spaceman,
and Pearl can be a Queen.
Jack can be a Giant
dressed in red and green.

Jasmine can be a Cowgirl,
and George can be a King.
Gaz can be a Wizard
with a magic ring.

Matt can be a Doctor,
and Jazz can be a Nurse.
I will be a Teacher
reading out this verse.

Guess Who?

My vest is blue,
    my socks are red.
        A purple hat
            sits on my head.

My shorts are pink,
    my shirt is black.
        Six silver stars
            shine on my back.

My gloves are gold,
    my shoes are brown.
    Who am I?

A circus clown!

15

I'm a Rabbit

I'm a Rabbit
   rolled in a ball.

I'm a Horse
   jumping a wall.

I'm a Mouse
   nibbling at cheese.

I'm a Dog
   scratching its fleas.

I'm a Hen
   pecking at straw.

And I'm a Cat
   asleep on the floor.

The Autumn Leaves

In autumn
the trees wave in the wind
and the leaves come tumbling

down

down

down

down.

Here they come
hundreds and thousands of leaves
in yellow, red,

hazel

gold

and

chocolate brown.

A Week of Winter Weather

On Monday icy rain poured down
and flooded drains all over town.

Tuesday's gales bashed elm and ash:
dead branches came down with a crash.

On Wednesday bursts of hail and sleet.
No one walked along our street.

Thursday stood out clear and calm,
but the sun was paler than my arm.

Friday's frost that bit your ears
was cold enough to freeze your tears.

Saturday

Saturday's sky was ghostly grey.
We smashed ice on the lake today.

Sunday

Christmas Eve was Sunday ... and
snow fell like foam across the land.

Our Snowman

Wow, fatter and fatter and fatter he grows!
We give him coal eyes and a red carrot nose.
He has a thick scarf for the North Wind that blows
and slippers to warm his cold toes,
       his cold toes,
        and slippers to warm
       his cold toes!

Up the Wooden Hill

Yawn!
to bed.
wooden hill
up the
going
sleepyhead,
dreamy
I'm a
Ted.
to one-armed
holding on
to bed,
wooden hill
Up the
Yawn!   ← (Start here)

Counting to Sleep

One. Two. Three. Four.
Five. Six. And Seven more.
Counting spiders,
counting flies,
counting rabbits,
     close

               your

                         eyes ...

One. Two. Three. Four.
Five. Six. And Seven more.
Counting horses,
counting sheep,
counting seagulls,
     fall

               asleep ...

What do you think?

Look at the poem 'In My Garden'.
Can you find the words that rhyme
with 'goes'?

Read the poem 'Playtime'.
What do you and your
friends do at playtime?

Can you remember
why the snowman
has slippers?

Read the poem 'Yellow Boots'.
Do you have a pair of favourite shoes?
What do you like to do in them?

Carers' and teachers' notes

- Talk to your child about why some of the words in the poems are in **bold** type. (For emphasis when reading aloud.)
- Together, learn the poem 'Stroke the Cat' (page 4). Encourage your child to add the hand actions while reciting the poem.
- 'Climb the Mountain' (page 8) is a shape poem. Help your child to write his/her own shape poem about, for example, a Christmas tree, a house or a snake.
- Read 'Animal Chat' (page 9). Encourage your child to make the animal noises as you read. Help your child to write his/her own version of the poem (it does not have to rhyme), featuring different animals and the noises that they make.
- Practise reading 'My Dog's First Poem' (page 10) 'in a dog's voice'. Ask your child what a doggy voice would sound like. Have fun with your child, writing a funny poem in the style of 'My Dog's First Poem'. Help him/her to choose another pet. Make the poem rhyme and remember to get the last rhyme in each verse wrong!
- Read 'Dressing Up' (page 14). Help your child to write a further verse for the poem, using the names of his/her friends and thinking of people/animals that those friends could dress up as.
- Read the riddle, 'Guess Who?' (page 15). What is the answer to the riddle? Help your child to write a riddle about a pet or a person he/she knows.
- 'I'm a Rabbit' (page 16) is an action poem. Encourage your child to act out the poem as you read it.
- Read the poem 'A Week of Winter Weather' (page 18). Encourage your child to write his/her own 'My Week' poem, about all the interesting things that he/she has been doing at home and at school. For example: 'On Monday I played with my friend/I hoped the day would never end.'
- Look at pages 22 and 23 with your child and discuss possible answers to the questions. Use your child's answer to the question about his/her favourite shoes as the basis for writing a new poem, based on 'Yellow Boots'.